DO THE RIGHT THING, DO IT ALL THE TIME

75 SUCCESS SECRETS LISTED FOR FAST REFERENCE

FRANK LEIGH

Can and Will Books

Published by Can and Will Books
canandwillbooks.com
An imprint of iCrew Digital Publishing

Cover design by DJ Rogers
justwritedesign.com

ISBN-13: 978-1946739032 (Can and Will Books)

ISBN-10: 1946739030

❀ Created with Vellum

CONTENTS

INTRODUCTION

This book is for you up and coming people that are starting to succeed in life and also for people that are struggling, frustrated, wondering why their success is taking so long and looking for answers. My hope is that it will be a tool to give you some very quick insight and a feeling of empowerment to speed up your success.

This book reads like a reference list of 75 of the best success laws and principles, taken from wisdom passed down by people that have come before us. Secret maybe, maybe not, but if you haven't been exposed to some of these ideas before then an "Ah-Ha" moment or two probably awaits. Hopefully the reader will be enlightened as to why one person is a great success and another person is still struggling. Each secret is only one or two pages long, and designed to be read in just a minute or two. The idea is to read one secret in a minute, but then think about that secret for a bit, and decide for yourself if anything is true or helpful about that secret. Because the power to succeed resides in what you think about; then where you direct your energy, what you do, and the ability you gain along the way.

These secret's mixed with a little thought, and your unique

interpretation can give you inner power. This power becomes thoughts and beliefs that will guide your life. This is exactly the kind of power required to succeed. You may not know that you have the power within you. This book reveals the power within you and the fact that success has been close beside you all along.

SECRET 1 - ACTION

Words, ideas, and beliefs are alive and working in your heart, but the power is released for all to see when you take action.

By your actions, you speak to the world. People hear your actions loud and clear. With your actions, you demonstrate what you believe, and people see and hear you clearly.

When you act, you trigger forces in the world that add energy to your power in that direction. This energy is a secret power and can work for you or against you. For example, if you act out of fear, you are demonstrating that you believe the thing you fear is too much for you, and it will be. However, if you act with courage and with faith that you can overcome whatever you fear, then the energy helps make it true. By your actions, you show the world what you are saying, believing, and seeing, and the energy that surrounds your intentions (one way or another) will help.

When you act, things get done, so develop a sense of urgency. When you feel like you should be taking action, that is the time to start. If you wait and think about it, you will talk yourself out of it.

You will be able to handle it, one way or another. Just decide and start. "Once begun is half done," as the saying goes. Move forward, and keep moving forward. Momentum is power. Every action counts, and every action adds up. Persistent action compounds, and compounding action is extreme power. Persistent, focused action is extreme power.

SECRET 2 - AMBITION

Your ambition is *your* ambition, not somebody else's. If you dream of achieving something great, don't let others talk you out of it just because they're not ambitious or they don't believe in you. It's hard to continue with the dream when you have naysayers around and you're frustrated, because you have not yet achieved your goal. Do not fear what others think or say. Feel good about your progress, and keep believing that you have such ambition for a reason. If you believe you can do it, you can. With perseverance, you will succeed if you just don't give up. Ambition is a source of power for you in the middle of the long, lonely path to success. Greatness awaits the ambitious.

SECRET 3 - ASSOCIATIONS

D on't underestimate the power of associations and the influence other people have on you. The people you spend time with effect your thinking, attitude, opinions, actions, and even how you dress and talk. Who you associate with matters.

If you surround yourself with the wrong sort of people—negative people, cynics, complainers, and unmotivated, undisciplined, unhappy people—they will automatically bring you down.

If you surround yourself with the right kind of people, people who have a positive outlook, are prosperous, disciplined, focused, growing, motivated, upbeat people—they will automatically lift you up.

If you choose to limit your exposure to the wrong people, and hang out with the right people, you will automatically raise your game to a higher level.

SECRET 4 - ATTITUDE

People love people with a good attitude. However it's hard to keep a good attitude when you're faced with one challenge after another. Staying optimistic and feeling good require a little focus and attention.

To help you maintain a good attitude, surround yourself with positive, happy people. Read positive things. Listen to music, or watch media that is uplifting and relaxing. Whistle or hum while you work. Sing a song in your heart, and speak happy words. Continually look for the good in things. Count your blessings. Tell yourself that challenges are good for you, because they make you stronger. Keep the big picture in perspective, and remember how time changes things. Smile, and the world will smile back.

It takes focus and attention, sometimes more than you expect, but your attitude is something you can control. Practice makes perfect. If you pay attention to your attitude and try to guide it in the right direction, you will be stronger and more successful.

SECRET 5 - BUSINESS

Owning a business is one of the most effective ways to become wealthy. You can create a business out of almost any activity that provides products or services to other people.

If people are willing to pay you for making or selling a product or providing a service, you can do it one time, then another, and if you keep doing it, you will have a business.

Kids can start with a lemonade stand, tutoring younger kids, babysitting, mowing lawns, or many other common activities.

Adults can take a product or service and provide that product or service on a larger scale, getting helpers (employees) to assist them in serving more and more people. The more people you help with your product or service, the more money you will make.

Business owners who serve a lot of people have found it is one of the most effective ways to become wealthy.

SECRET 6 - CHANGE

The world is changing constantly. To achieve success, you must be open minded, flexible, and willing to change. If what you're doing is not working, adjust your course. We are learning constantly, growing and evolving as we go. We take in new information, and with it, we become even better than before.

It is easy to keep things the same and stay in your comfort zone. Change is difficult, but the secret is; if you always do what is easy, you will become weak.

Change often requires that you endure uncomfortable feelings, but those feelings are necessary to grow into something new. So, if you need or want to change, embrace the uncomfortable feeling with the knowledge that, through it, a work is being done in you. The sooner you accept the uncomfortable feeling and let it run its course, the sooner you will become comfortable again and can enjoy the change. If you fight the uncomfortable feeling, you will merely prolong it, and you may even need to start over.

The world is changing constantly, and so are we. Be the best you can be, and do things as best as you can, but keep improving as you go. Not only will your world become better, so will you.

SECRET 7 - CHOICES

Success is rarely an overnight occurrence. For most people, success comes as a result of a series of good choices made consistently over an extended period.

Such choices move you closer and closer to success little by little. Every now and then, one of those good choices thrusts you to a new level of success, and then it's back to little by little until you spring up to another level.

Good choices made consistently over a long period of time is the way most successful people succeed.

If you make the right choices, success is guaranteed.

SECRET 8 - CONSCIENCE

Your conscience is the little voice in your head that tells you what is right and what is wrong. When you argue with your conscience or ignore it and do something that doesn't feel right, it will disturb your peace of mind. It's hard enough to make all of the everyday decisions we encounter in life, and we need all the help we can get. Your conscience is a guiding force that helps you decide the right things to do, day in and day out. No one knows the source of this little voice; perhaps it is God himself. Whatever the source of this sense of right and wrong, you ignore it at your peril. Tune in to it, and use it as your guide. If you do the right thing consistently, you are guaranteed to have far more long-term success, peace, and happiness in every area of your life.

SECRET 9 - CONSISTENCY

The moral of the old story about the race between the tortoise and the hare is that slow and steady wins the race.

This story is true in a sense. You can win in the long run by being consistent. You don't have to be the strongest or fastest; you just have to be the most consistent. Many people start out strong and do way more than you in the beginning, and it seems like they are winning the race. But they often burn out over the long run, lose focus and stop. If you, on the other hand, continue moving toward the finish line, eventually, you will pass the point where others stopped, and you will go on to win—not because you are faster but because you are more consistent.

You can apply consistency to virtually every area of your life.

SECRET 10 - DECISION

The secret is; when you decide, you force life in the direction of your choices.

Your ability to decide things is one of the biggest forces that will help you overcome procrastination and move in the direction you want to go.

Once you're able to decide, you can move forward. If you analyze your decisions too much, waiting for everything to be perfect and crystal clear, you will get stuck. It takes courage to make a decision when conditions are not perfect. You must be willing to make a decision, think on your feet, and move forward, ready to figure out the details as you go. Once you decide where you are going and what you plan to do, you can swiftly and decisively come up with a plan for how to get there. When you have the plan, then you can act on it swiftly and decisively. Your decisive action is what counts most. If your decision or the plan turns out to be flawed, adjust, learn, and make a better decision or plan. When your decision is firm, and you are totally committed, the world will get out of your way to enable you to achieve your goal.

If you are not committed, your force will be weak. The stronger your decision, the easier it will be to commit, because the spirit of the decision in your heart will help you fight, do what you want to do, and persevere. To make your decision strong, get clear in your mind about why you believe in it. With that belief, commit yourself completely, no turning back, and move forward in faith. Back up your decision with persistence, determination, and patience, and you will be unstoppable.

The truly inspiring thing about a decision is that it is within your control. You can follow your own decision; you don't need to include others if they don't agree. The more you control your decisions, the more you will be able to force life in the direction you choose.

The power of decision is strong, and that power is yours.

SECRET 11 - DO THE RIGHT THING

N othing will fall into place and work for your good in the long run unless you do the right thing and do it all the time.

Life gives you one test after another to see what you will do. If you make bad choices and do bad things, bad things will happen to you.

When you realize that everything you do affects everything that happens to you later on, then you will gain a measure of control over your life. The law of nature that balances the good and bad you do with the good and bad you receive will always reward or punish you in some way for the choices you make and the things you do. The effects of what you do today may not show up until later, but they will show up one way or another. We don't know how things will come back on us, so we must always do the good, truthful things all the time. Then the unknown repercussions will be for us and not against us. If you don't have an account of good things headed your way, you will struggle, but you may never know why. A law of nature balances the good and the bad you do with the good and bad that happen to you. When you do the right thing, and do it all the time, your life will get better and better and better.

SECRET 12 - EGO

A controlled ego can help you; an uncontrolled ego can hurt you.

It is healthy to feel good about yourself and who you are. The self-confidence boost and belief in yourself give you the resolve to begin a thing and see it through. This is good.

Problems occur when healthy pride (satisfaction in what you have achieved) turns into arrogance. If you think you can do no wrong, then you lose the ability to consider other points of view. If you dismiss others without consideration, going to any length to prove yourself right, nobody will want to be around you, people will not help you, and you will miss many opportunities.

Strive to keep a healthy ego and an open mind. Be confident, but if light is shed on a subject, revealing an error in your thinking, be the first to admit your mistake. Laughing at yourself, being humble, and giving others credit for their ideas is an endearing quality.

Be confident, but be ready to adjust your thinking, and you will go far.

SECRET 13 - EMOTIONS

E motions move you. Your emotions are a driving force that sweep you up and move your actions along like a tidal wave.

Emotions can power you to incredible achievement or colossal mistakes. The passion contained in emotions can land you in jail or help you obtain the object of your dreams.

Your emotions partially control your actions, so you must be aware of when they are affecting you. If you are not aware that your emotions are affecting you, you will become like a puppet at the mercy of whatever direction the wave of emotion wants to take you, which could be right onto the rocks. However, if you are aware of your emotions, then you can steer your actions like a surfer riding a wave. You will still be affected, but at least you will know it is happening and be able to channel your passion toward becoming a super achiever.

How you feel about something brings out your emotions, and your emotions bring about a reaction that moves you. The emotions of love, joy, happiness, fear, anger, sadness, and any other strong feeling will move you. For example, if you get scared, you may jump with a power you didn't know you had. Once you realize you're scared, then you can plan your next move and channel your fear into power to execute a plan. Alternatively, if you realize you love doing something, that passion can be the driving force needed to pick you up and sweep you along to achieve that very thing.

SECRET 14 - ENTHUSIASM

E nthusiasm is a force that will inspire you to do more, be more, achieve more, and carry on longer than you could without it.

Motivation is the reason why you want to do something, but enthusiasm is the force that backs up motivation. Enthusiasm says, "I want to do this. I will do this. Let's get it done. Let's do it. I'm excited to do this. Let's keep going." Enthusiasm comes from agreeing with and believing in the reasons you want to do something. If you don't believe in the reasons, then your heart will not be in it, and your actions will lack force. However, if you believe strongly in what you are doing, then your enthusiasm will be high, and it will empower you to do it with increased focus, determination, persistence, power, and joy.

If you can go through life doing things with more enthusiasm, your heart will be in it, things will seem easier, and you will experience far more success.

SECRET 15 - FAILURE

Failure is an event, not a person.

Every time you fail at something, you have the opportunity to learn to do it better or differently next time. So, go ahead and fail quickly and often so you can learn how to succeed.

Failure does not hold us back. It just makes us smarter and stronger so we can try again. Fear of failure is what keeps us from trying in the first place and limits our accomplishments.

Just because many things don't work perfectly the first time you try them does not mean the situation is permanent. No failure is permanent. If you look for something good in every setback, obstacle, and temporary failure and learn from it, you will be better equipped to try again. Failure only becomes permanent when you stop trying.

You can learn from your mistakes and the mistakes of others. If you see what messed up someone else's life, take it as a warning. Learn from their experience, so you don't make the same mistake.

If you fail at something, don't whine and cry and blame others. Pick yourself up and ask, "What can I learn from this to do better next time?" Then turn it around, go back to work, and put it all together again if you have to, being careful not to make the same mistake twice. Sometimes the biggest failures turn out to be the biggest gifts, because they teach you the biggest lesson, enabling you to succeed.

Failure is an event, not a person.

SECRET 16 - FAITH

F aith is belief. Faith is when you believe in something or believe you can do something, even when there are no guarantees.

If everything was certain, you wouldn't need faith. In life, there are times when we don't have everything figured out, and we don't know what will happen, but we have to try to make sense of things and decide what to do anyway. At such times, you must choose to believe or not, in yourself or whatever is in question. It is your choice to believe or not to believe. What you believe in the face of uncertainty will determine what thoughts you have, what actions you take, and the life you create.

You can create faith by feeling in your imagination that what you want to believe, is real. Seeing or feeling it as real in your mind will give you confidence, trust, and belief. You can also create faith by repeating positive self-affirmations, instructions, or information in your mind until your subconscious mind accepts it. When the subconscious mind believes it, and has faith, a universe of possibilities will open up.

If you don't believe something is possible, your mind will close to the possibilities. If you believe something is possible, then faith in those possibilities will unlock your imagination, enabling you to see things and do things that you couldn't see or do before. Faith unlocks part of your brain, making more power available.

Circumstances and outcomes are often uncertain. We don't always have everything figured out, and we are not always strong enough or smart enough to know something for sure. It's easy to quit when you're unsure. Sometimes the only way to make sense of things or move forward when you're unsure is through faith. Faith is your courage, your guide, your hope, your insight, your protection, and your inspiration. Faith is your secret power to act in spite of fear and uncertainty; to make a decision, move forward, and succeed.

Don't say, "I'll believe it when I see it." Say, "I'll see it, because I believe it."

If you believe you can; you can.

If you believe you will; you will.

Do not underestimate the power of belief.

Do not underestimate a person who has faith.

SECRET 17 - FEAR

If you are facing death, stand strong. God is available for people in need. Do not underestimate the power of prayer. Use examples of situations similar to yours that worked out, to give you hope. Believe things will get better, then act on that belief. Do the best you can, get the best help you can, and trust that a positive outcome is possible. When you act on faith that things will get better, it activates God, and you will have extra power. Things tend to work out over time. Everything will be okay.

If nobody's going to die because of whatever you're afraid of, then keep your fear in perspective. Many others have it worse. It is not a crisis; it is only a situation. Situations are temporary. Relax; you will get through it.

Have courage. Don't be afraid to make mistakes or be embarrassed, because those times make you more memorable. They make people laugh, and they enable people to relate to you, because nobody's perfect.

Have courage; you don't need to fear failure. Failure is okay, because we learn and become stronger, smarter, and better equipped to try again. Everybody fails at things; it is part of life. Just learn from it and try again.

You can develop courage even when you are afraid and there are no guarantees. Think to yourself over and over, "I can do it! I can do it! It will be okay! I t will be okay!" Think and talk about only positive outcomes, and decide that even if the outcome is negative, you will be able to accept it and deal with it one way or another. Eventually, with enough repetition of positive thoughts, your subconscious will allow you to move forward.

To master your fears, move forward despite of them. You can build up courage like a muscle by repeatedly forcing yourself to take courageous action.

When fear is your motivating force, you can take incredible action.

SECRET 18 - FINANCIAL FREEDOM

If you stopped working today, would you still have enough money coming in to pay the bills and do what you want to do and live comfortably forever? If you can say "yes" to that question, then you have achieved financial freedom.

The secret is; that it can be done. Probably before the age of retirement if you start now.

The first key is to keep your expenses low. If you have low or almost no expenses, then you don't need much money do you? The fewer expenses you have the less money it takes to achieve financial freedom. The trap many of us fall into is trying to keep up with other people's lifestyles. Just because you see someone else get fancy things does not mean you should run out and buy such things, too. People who try to keep up the appearance of being wealthy are often spending at their maximum and are only one or two paychecks away from financial disaster. Just because you can buy it, does not mean you should. Your desire to feel financially strong needs to be greater than your desire to show off with fancy stuff.

The second key to achieving financial freedom is to increase your income while keeping your lifestyle expenses the same. Remember, just because you start making more does not mean you need to spend more. You are smart enough to find ways to make extra money over time.

The third key to achieving financial freedom is to invest your extra money into paying down debt, building an emergency reserve account, maxing out your 401k or retirement account contributions, and buying income-producing investments, such as rental properties, that pay for themselves and make you money. It is okay to take on debt if the debt is for an investment that pays for itself and produces income. The crucial point when putting your extra money to work for your financial freedom plan is to spend it only on things that save or make you money.

The fourth key to achieving financial freedom is to maintain this lifestyle and focus for many years— until you have little or no debt, a large emergency reserve account, and enough income being produced by your investments that you don't have to work anymore. At that point, you can keep working or not or buy some things to show off or not. It is up to you, because you have achieved financial freedom.

Some strategies are: If you are married and both you and your spouse are working, you can live off one person's income and use the other income for your financial freedom plan. If you have only one income, then live off half of what you earn and invest the other half in your financial freedom plan. You can also get a second job or side business and use that income for your financial freedom plan. When you pay off debt, you can keep making the payment, but now instead of the payment gong to the debt, it can be a monthly payment into your financial freedom plan.

If you focus on a plan and stick with it, given enough time, you will gain financial freedom.

SECRET 19 - FOCUS

You will look like a genius if you develop the ability to focus single-mindedly on one thing at a time and persevere without diversion until completion.

You can learn this skill by keeping focused on the small tasks, like doing the dishes, until finished. This one skill of being able to put your head down and focus on your work until it's done can change your life.

Successful people don't have time to worry about what others say, think or do, because successful people are way too busy trying to keep the focus on their own success.

The secret is; there is a direct relationship between how focused you are on a goal and how rapidly that goal becomes a reality.

Focus simplifies things. Maybe you make things simple, or maybe you really are a genius.

SECRET 20 - FORGIVENESS

We get mentally stuck in life sometimes, because we keep thinking about some bad thing that happened in our past. We re-live the event by playing it over and over again in our mind. The emotions and bad feelings of the event keep hurting us and distracting us from moving forward, to a happy life.

We have all had people in our lives that have wronged us, or we may have done things we regret. The problem is, things can't always be made right; and what's done is done. We cannot go back, and others that have hurt us cannot go back and have a do-over. We can only learn from the experience and do things differently and better starting now.

Forgiveness is the secret tool; to get past hurt and regret, and make change. When you forgive yourself and others, you are not saying the hurt was okay, or that you want the same thing to happen again. What you are saying is, what's done is done, nobody's perfect, people are often misguided, and don't really know what they are doing. Even if others are still misguided, I am no longer misguided and no longer a victim. I will not be stuck in the past with thoughts of ill will towards the misguided. I accept—"it is what it is". I will change as needed, be a little stronger a little wiser but with forgiveness, I am moving on, back to a happy life.

SECRET 21 - GIVING BACK

Providing support, helping others, and giving back is something you can do almost every day. Even if you have only a little, you can still give an encouraging word to a family member, a sympathetic ear to your spouse, or share a smile, a laugh, or compliment with your co-worker.

We work so hard to help ourselves, but when we are blessed, it is never completely our own doing. Others always play a part in our blessing. Being a blessing to others when we can is the right thing to do. Provide support, help others, and giving back with no expectation of reward or recognition. Do it just because it's a good thing to do. This is the true spirit of giving.

The secret of giving is this: When you give, you get back much more than you ever put out. The more you give, the more you get. It is a law of nature.

SECRET 22 - GOALS

Strong personal goals are a secret power source. A strong personal goal is something you can see in your mind and desire so strongly it is almost like an obsession. The more personal the goal is and the bigger the reasons why you want to achieve it, the more your motivational power will be amplified. It will give you increased courage, focus, decisiveness, willpower, determination, discipline, endurance, resilience, creativity, and the insights required to overcome the inevitable setbacks and obstacles you will encounter along the path and continue for as long as it takes to achieve your goal.

Determine exactly what your goals are, envision them clearly in your mind, and how they would impact your life if achieved. Then write your goals out on paper. Having a goal in mind is good for the big picture, but writing it down so you can see it frees up your mind from the big picture so you can release your creativity. It enables you to work through far more complex details and come up with a workable plan. To give written goals more power, read them daily, and make the picture in your mind clearer and clearer until you develop an unshakable belief that you will achieve your goal.

Every goal comes at a price. Determine what price you must pay to achieve your goal, and then resolve to pay it. The goal doesn't happen by itself. What you put in is what you get out, and you must pay the price in advance.

When practical ideas and plans for what you need to do become evident, act on them right away. Then keep moving forward. The details of what you need to do will become clearer with each step you take. Learn every lesson you can from the good and the bad you encounter along the way. When it becomes clear that you need to revise your plans, accept it and revise them immediately.

Resolve to keep moving forward no matter what. Many people hit obstacles and temporary defeat and stop a few feet from the finish line or one day too soon. Recognize that there will be challenges along the way that you must figure out how to overcome. Maybe you need to get expert council to overcome an obstacle, or maybe you need to come at it from a different angle, or perhaps you just need to keep pushing for as long as it takes. Persistence is a state of mind that you must cultivate and employ. You can cultivate persistence by establishing habits, such as staying on task and finishing the job, blocking out discouraging influences, letting in encouraging people, and strengthening your desire to achieve your goals, almost to the point of obsession. If you convince yourself there is no going back, that you are all in, moving forward no matter what for as long as it takes, then things will mysteriously fall into place. Obstacles will be swept out of the way. You will become an unstoppable force.

Provided your goals are built upon truth and doing what's right and benefiting all who are involved, the unexplainable power of coincidence, insights, opportunities, and connections will show up and give you that little extra help you need to do something great.

You are destined to do great things, and those great things start out as goals.

SECRET 23 - GOD

Who knows for sure? Every person can decide for themselves. This is only my humble opinion. The more fear and uncertainty you encounter in life, the more you tend to look to God for guidance, wisdom, strength, courage, and protection. I didn't always believe in God, but in trying to get through hard times and understand life I looked for God's guidance, I came to believe that God exists. God is in us, and all things, all around us, and ever present. It seems like God likes to show his power most when we feel our own power is not enough. That's when we tune in and God's miracles are visible. We can tune in only by wanting to believe. We are limited only by our lack of belief. When I began to believe in God, I felt like I grew another level in my development, and with that new level came new insights, understandings, convictions, acceptance, courage, resolve, and power. I think belief in God unlocks another part of the brain, the part that is able to trust that God will make a way even if you don't see a way. The more you look, the more you see. The more you see, the more you trust and believe. If you trust God and believe he will help you, then you will have the courage to do far more than you would otherwise. Your success will be far greater with God. I think believing in God is about trusting that God will make a way, tuning in to God's guidance, and trusting that guidance to help you do the right thing all the time.

For the Lord God is our light and protector. He gives us grace and glory. No good thing will the Lord withhold from those who do what is right. (Psalm 84:11, NLT)

"Don't get tired of doing what's right, for in due season, you will reap if you just don't give up"(Galatians 6:9)

SECRET 24 - GOING WITH
THE FLOW

One secret to success in life is to recognize that many invisible forces in life move in definite directions. If you go with the flow of the good forces, they will push you along, making everything easier for you. If you go against those forces, it is like fighting against a headwind all the time. Go with the good flow. Let the force be with you. Some forces will help put you in the jet stream of life and make everything easier. For example, if your attitude is positive and optimistic, the force will be with you.

Maintain your peace. A peaceful mind flows in a position of power.

More examples: Build momentum. Once you get moving, you tend to stay moving. Practice self-discipline. Do what you should be doing; the flow goes that way. Remain focused. What you focus on grows and comes to life. Seek goodness. Do good, and good things will happen. Love, and you will be loved. Hold onto hope. Hope creates possibilities. Have faith. Faith gives you the courage to act and lets the invisible interact.

Not everything is visible, but that doesn't mean it doesn't exist.

SECRET 25 - GRATITUDE

Be happy and grateful for all the good things in your life, and plenty more coming your way.

When you are down, discouraged, or weary, gratitude is a proven mindset to bring you back to happiness, making you feel positive and energized. Be thankful for all that you have. All the little things add up to a lot. You may not have everything you want right now, but you have plenty for which to be thankful. Say to yourself, "I am happy and grateful for all the good things in my life, and plenty more are coming my way." Repeat this in your mind as you think about it, and not only will you see things change for the better, the secret is; good things will actually be drawn to you. Gratitude is powerful, and you have that power.

SECRET 26 - HABITS

We all have habits, good and bad. Think of a habit you have, such as brushing your teeth at a regular time each day. Now imagine that you have the power to create another habit you want, adding it to your routine, just like brushing your teeth. Do you have that power? Of course, yes!

Here's one way to do it: Think of what you want to add to your daily routine. Get a clear picture in your mind of all the reasons why you want to add that habit. Think of those reasons until it becomes a belief that you can, will, and must do it. Then do it once. Force yourself if you must, but do it once. After doing it, focus on the feelings of satisfaction, self-esteem, and happiness you feel as a result. Then repeat the process. Think of all the reasons why, do it once again, and focus on the good feelings you experience. Hang in there, force yourself through this process many times. You will notice that every time it becomes easier, and eventually you will not be forcing yourself but actually looking forward to the new habit. Shortly after that, it will become automatic, just like brushing your teeth. When a habit becomes automatic, it is like a secret autopilot keeping your life on course. You can eliminate bad habits using the same method, get strong reasons to stop, force yourself not to do it once, then again, and focus on how it gets easier every time.

You have the power to create or eliminate any habit you want.

SECRET 27 - HAPPINESS

If you focus on happy thoughts and surround yourself with happy, upbeat, positive influences, those thoughts will become more dominant, making you happier.

Think about happy things you are grateful for, and those things can become your foundation of go-to thoughts to remember whenever life is hard.

By understanding that you are the biggest influence on yourself, that you decide almost everything about you, you can make choices that move you in direction that makes you feel good about yourself. You may not have everything you want yet, but you can develop a sense of control and direction over your life. Control makes you happier.

Bad things happen sometimes, and things don't always make sense. But you don't always have to find the reasons or make sense of bad things. The key is to get past them as quickly as possible by settling the matter in your mind one way or another. Forgive, forget, deal with it, put it behind you, let it go, and move forward, getting back to your happy thoughts.

People get blinded and obsessed by one bad thing happening in life and forget all the good things. Remember most things are good.

The few things that are not good usually turn out to be easier to deal with than you thought. Even the very difficult things work out in the long run.

Think about the thousands of decisions you must make every day, from deciding what pair of shoes to wear to figuring out what to eat. Most decisions we make turn out fine, but what are the chances that every single decision and event is going to be perfect? The answer? Zero. Therefore, don't be too surprised or too upset when things don't go as exactly as planned; just learn from it. It is only one decision or event in the millions of decisions and events you will have to deal with in your lifetime. Remember most things are still good.

Happiness is a choice. You can decide ahead of time to be happy no matter what happens. Then it will be easier to remember and focus on the reasons why you are happy. Think, say, and look for "happy" until you feel it and believe it.

When you are happy, let it grow. This is an advanced frame of mind, because the natural tendency is to focus on the bad things, but when things are going well, dwell on them. Focus on how things get better and better. Let the good things grow. Look for happiness, expect it, and you will find it.

Let it grow—this is a secret key to life. When we think about something, we are planting a seed. If we continue to think about that thing, it is like watering and fertilizing the seed until it grows into a tree. Here is the secret: What you think about grows. What you stop thinking about dies. You can grow a mental tree of happiness just by thinking a lot about why you are happy. You can also kill off the unhappy trees by refusing to give them your attention. You can take control by mentally watering the happiness tree on a regular basis.

Happiness is contagious. If you exude happiness by saying and thinking happy things and acting happily, others will pick up on it, and you will make them happy, too. Also, if you hang out with happy people, it will rub off on you. Happiness is like rocket fuel for success.

SECRET 28 - HEALTH

Is there a secret miracle something that can keep you feeling young and strong and at the same time make you smarter, give you more energy, and prevent all kinds of health issues? Yes! It's called exercise.

We all have the excuse that we don't have enough time, but I submit to you that any time you put into exercise you get back many times over in the form of better mental focus, more energy, a feeling of being younger and stronger and more able, and that leads to higher performance and endurance at work and in other areas of life. Good health enables you to get more done in less time, and it makes things easier to do. Better performance in life leads to good things. So, you must exercise as part of your success plan. The time invested will come back to you many times over, and you will probably add many good years to your life as well. Now that is a good return on time invested. You don't have to spend a lot of time or do anything ridiculously difficult; just get moving. If you haven't exercised in a while, start with five minutes a day, and see where that leads you. Be intentional, and make it a lifestyle.

What you put into your body is another major factor that determines good health. You don't have to be a chemist to understand that some foods and drinks are bad for you, and others are good for you. Some food and drinks give momentary pleasure, but make you feel not so good an hour or a day later for one reason or another. If you know what is good, stock up on that, so it is most convenient, and keep the bad stuff out of the pantry and hard to get. We are far from perfect, but we can take a little more control of what we put into our bodies and as a result, feel a little younger, stronger, more able, and live longer. Is it another miracle?

Sleep is another major factor for good health. Sleep washes the brain clean of toxins every night, making you clear headed and smart and energizing you for the day ahead. The better you sleep, the more you will get done, and the better you will feel and that leads to success.

You are the one controls the secret miracle; you are the one that brings good health to you.

SECRET 29 - HOPE

Hope is real.
Hope is not just wishing something will happen. Hope is related to trust and confident expectation.

When you have hope, you are not escaping from reality or problems and just sitting there wishing for the best. Hope gives you optimism, encouragement and power to get up, get moving, and carry on to do what you can.

When there is no real assurance in your circumstances, you can use hope. Hope is a real power.

SECRET 30 - IDEAS

S uccess is often as close as a good idea.

If you are looking for ideas, you will find them.

Ideas start businesses, sell products and services, supply needs, and solve problems.

Most problems can be solved with a good idea.

When you have a good idea, write it down so you remember it.

Good ideas can be drawn from bits and pieces of information hidden in your mind, that jump out at you, or from seeking and finding a thing that inspires.

Two or more people who brainstorm together to come up with ideas are more powerful than one person by him or herself.

Great things begin by dreaming up an idea. If the dream is practical, it can become a reality by mixing it with inspiration, faith, and persistent thought and action.

You may have to push to get an idea started, but then the idea will begin to push you, sweeping away opposition and empowering you to success.

Success is often as close as a good idea.

SECRET 31 - IMAGINATION

The imagination is a place and a thing, a place where anything is possible and a thing that likes to create. It is a private place in your mind where you can dream about, think about, and do anything.

Your imagination can be a frivolous, fun place to let your true personality and thoughts run wild, but your imagination can also be a serious workshop if you are trying to create something. Your imagination is where you can take every thought you ever had and put them together in a totally different way to create something new.

Sometimes you are trying to create and using all the bits and pieces you can think of but get stuck for a long time on the missing piece that you need for the creation. Then from your subconscious mind or intuition or out of the blue, the missing piece pops into your imagination. You have no idea where the missing piece came from, but it feels almost magical. You can use the power of your imagination to solve problems, make plans, and to create new ideas and things. There is something magical about a place where anything is possible and a thing that likes to create.

Don't underestimate the dreamers.

SECRET 32 - INTEGRITY

The secret is; people value honesty and sincerity more than almost every other virtue.

If you can't be trusted, you will be given very little. If you can be trusted, you will have great success.

It takes a long time of doing the right thing in every situation for people to trust you. People do not believe what you say, but they watch carefully and believe what you do. Set a good example, and let your actions speak for you.

SECRET 33 - INTELLIGENCE

E verybody has some genius in them.
Do not judge your intelligence by your ability, or inability, to pass tests in subjects that do not interest you or poor grades you might have had in school. Judge your intelligence by your ability to move toward your goals and excel at things that do interest you.

There are book smarts, and there are street smarts. One is not necessarily better than the other. Having a little of each will probably give you the best results. For example, a college degree might help open a door to get a job, but hard work and responsible choices are what help you keep the job and advance.

Whatever knowledge, experience, and abilities you have, use them to size up your situation and the options available that will move you toward your goals. Then trust your judgement, and choose the best options available to you. Work hard, keep making the best possible choices, reflect on your experiences (both good and bad), learn, improve, adjust as necessary, and continue to move toward your goals for as long as it takes. If you achieve your goals, who's the real genius?

Just because someone knows more about a subject than you do does not mean that person is smarter than you. He or she may be a genius at one thing, but you have an aptitude for something else. We are all equally smart but in different ways. If there is some genius in all of us, then your ability to move in the direction of your goals and interests is how you will make your personal genius evident. You have genius in you.

SECRET 34 - KINDNESS

K indness is treating people around you well. It is showing people that you are genuine, friendly, generous, merciful, empathetic, and understanding. Kindness is treating people with respect, listening, speaking gentle words, offering a helping hand or a gift, or just being nice.

If you build a reputation for genuine kindness, you will put people at ease, and they will feel safe around you. You will enable them to relax and feel more comfortable.

A kind word can change a person's life. Small acts of kindness are not wasted. A touch, a smile, an honest compliment, and being genuinely good and kind will improve your life and the lives of those around you. You can set the example even when others can't or won't.

Having knowledge or power does not mean you should be harsh and unforgiving of others who are at a disadvantage. A real sign of greatness is when a person with power is so secure that he or she can be gentle, merciful, and kind to all.

SECRET 35 - KNOWLEDGE

Is knowledge power? Knowing something is good, but it is not power unless you use that knowledge in some way. So, while it may be fun to learn general knowledge about all kinds of things, it is not the same as focusing on a particular aspect of your life and education that will lead to more success in a specific area of your life. The secret is; if you learn specialized knowledge that you can use to enhance your career, your goals, your health, and your happiness and then use that knowledge to make better decisions take better actions and improve those areas, then you have true power.

The good news is, you don't have to become an expert in every subject; however, you do need to become good at knowing where to find the specialized knowledge you require when you need it. If you know where to find it or who to ask when the knowledge is required, then that is power.

If you have a person or group of people you can team up with to brainstorm ideas; that is power. Because you will always have more ideas, better insights, and more useful results than you can obtain on your own.

Keep learning about the aspects of your life, and you will keep improving your ability to act intelligently.

Knowledge that leads to intelligent action is power.

SECRET 36 - LAW OF ATTRACTION

The law of attraction says that things attract other things that are like them. Like gravity pulling an object to itself.

If you want to draw things that you desire closer to you, recognize that thoughts have gravitational qualities, and then choose and direct your thoughts as if you were aiming a mental magnet at the things you want.

Thoughts stimulate the brain and will attract similar thoughts. One thought will mysteriously attract another. Thoughts lead to plans, plans lead to action, and action leads to attracting what you want.

The more you think about something, the stronger the law of attraction becomes. If you hold the thought in your mind long enough, somehow things will fall into place, and you will find a way to take action. You will probably attract the thing you are thinking about, for better or worse. So, make sure you aim your thoughts and control what you think about, because if you think about something you don't want, it will also be drawn to you. The law of attraction can work for you or against you, and it will work even if you are unaware. So, choose the things you want to attract, and maintain your focus.

The gravitational force created by the law of attraction is subtle and invisible, but it grows like a snowball rolling down a hill, and reveals its power when held in place over time. This secret invisible force can be yours.

SECRET 37 - LEADERSHIP

Leaders know what they want and where they are going. That's why they are leaders. A leader's job is to make decisions quickly and firmly that move things in the direction required to achieve a goal.

Good leaders recognize the magnified power that is created when people team up to achieve a goal. A good leader inspires others to cooperate and pull together as a team for a common goal. The inspiration from a good leader comes not from fear and intimidation but from a demonstration of the leader's ability to lead well. A good leader will make clear to the advantages and benefits that can be obtained if his or her followers work together toward a common goal.

A good leader inspires and shows his or her ability to lead by communicating a definite vision and plan and by demonstrating courage and the ability to make firm decisions. A good leader inspires and shows his or her ability to lead by delegating the work to be done with a sense of fairness and justice. A good leader inspires and shows his or her ability to lead by taking responsibility for failures, adjusting plans quickly, if needed, and giving followers credit for successes. A good leader inspires and shows his or her ability to lead by being clear eyed, level headed, and having self-control in all situations. A good leader inspires and shows his or her ability to lead by treating people with respect and empathy and showing he or she cares about the welfare of his or her followers. A good leader inspires and demonstrates his or her ability to lead by having a pleasing personality, being willing to work harder than others, being humble, loyal, and, above all else, having unwavering integrity.

SECRET 38 - LOVE

How powerful is love?

Love is a force in life that will move heaven and earth to protect and provide for the welfare of loved ones.

If you act with love, the secret is: you will be in harmony with this force in life. You will be tapped into the power that can move heaven and earth. You will have more power, you will make better choices and you will do the right things.

You will still have disagreements and problems in life, but your power to understand, forgive, deal and act correctly will be strengthened. People will sense you acting out of love and will tend to love you back.

If you feel in your heart, some sort of love for the people and things around you, then you will automatically have this power from the universe on your side.

SECRET 39 - MAINTENANCE

It is not enough to acquire something good. Once you have achieved or obtained something good, then you must maintain it if you want to keep it. Sure, you probably know your car needs maintenance, but what about your body, relationships, skills, finances, and all the other good things in your life? For example, you might spend a lot of time getting your body into good shape, but to keep it that way, some regular maintenance is required. Relationships also deteriorate without regular attention. The same is true for virtually everything in life. We work so hard to bring good things into our lives, but often end up taking those things for granted. Small things attack and spoil what you have when you're not paying attention.

Pay attention to all the good things in your life, and with a glad heart, maintain all that goodness, and it will attract more.

SECRET 40 - MASTERMIND GROUP

A mastermind group is when two or more people get together to work in harmony toward the same goal by putting their thoughts together to come up with the best ideas, plans, and solutions to fix a problem or achieve a goal. Then they work together to implement those ideas to achieve the goal.

The power created by a mastermind group is more than just two or more people coming up with ideas. When you are truly in harmony with the group, a spiritual energy is created; giving you enhanced insight and ideas. Suddenly, you are able to come up with an idea you never would have thought of on your own. You didn't know you had it in you, but there it is; out of the blue, it just came to you, a great idea. The same happens for others in the group, and, all of a sudden, between you and your mastermind group, the best ideas, plans, and solutions come to light.

The secret is in the spiritual energy that manifests when like-minded people work together.

SECRET 41 - MONEY

Without money, your life is full of stress and anxiety. It is honorable for honest, hardworking men and women to strive for money to make a better life for themselves and their family. You should want to be prosperous, because prosperity is a good thing.

The secret is, making money and managing money are learnable skills. People who have a lot of money are not smarter than you and do not necessarily work harder than you, but they have learned some skills you may not have acquired. If you learn some money-making and money-handling skills and do what wealthy people do, you will have the same or better results.

Here are two basic things to get you started 1) Keep your expenses low and 2) increase your cash flow.

Becoming financially prosperous is as much about controlling expenses as it is about earning money. You are much more likely to be successful in business and your personal life if you keep your expenses low. If you start making more money, do not increase your lifestyle expenses. Keep the extra money and use it to pay off debt or create more cash flow.

Pay off debt. If you have debt, start by paying off the smallest debts first, and then use that momentum to pay off larger debts. If you have little or no debt, you will be stronger.

Learn to budget your money. Learn to say no to some expenses you don't really need, and make some short-term sacrifices for long-term gain. Make saving and investing part of your budget.

Cash flow is income that flows like a stream from one source or another into your life. You can have multiple streams from different sources. Some of the streams can be your job or your business, renting out a room in your house, buying and renting out houses, your spouse's income, stock dividends, or your side job or business. Do the extra work required to make the most of each revenue stream. For example, do the extra learning required to be the best at your job, to get promotions, and obtain raises.

Save money. When you save money each month, it makes you financially strong. The easiest way to do this is to have it deducted automatically from your income every month and put into an investment account.

Build a cash reserve for emergencies, such as if your income stops suddenly or you have a large, unexpected expense, but also in case a good moneymaking idea comes your way. Then you will be in a position to invest.

The key is to stop thinking about getting rich quickly and start thinking long term. Think about what you can do to set yourself up ten or twenty years in the future. Right now, you can create extra money every month by increasing your income, paying off debt, and minimizing your expenses. Then take the surplus money and use it to buy or invest in things that will grow over time and produce cash flow. Honest money is honorable and right. You are meant to be prosperous.

SECRET 42 - MOTIVATION

Motivation is anything that inspires you to want to do something.

Pay attention to the things that personally inspire you to act one way or another, so you will be able to identify what gets you excited, determined, and moving. Once you identify those motivators, you can use them to power you into action when you want to create or do something.

Strong motivators include love, sex, friendship, fear, money, help, embarrassment, pride, hope, kindness, curiosity, peace, or anything else that has meaning to you. That meaning is the power to act.

When you recognize what motivates you, keep it in mind as a driving force behind your action. This is how you tap into its power.

SECRET 43 - MOVING FORWARD

We may know where we want to go, but we will not get there unless we move forward.

Moving forward sounds obvious, but people often get stuck in place, because they are worried about the outcome.

You can look at the spot you want to go and see all kinds of obstacles in your path and be afraid you won't be able to make it through. As a result, you stay where you are. When others say, "It doesn't look easy" or "I don't think it will work," it just increases your anxiety.

The secret to moving forward is this: When you move forward, you find that most of the time the obstacles you were so worried about turn out to be a lot easier to overcome than you thought. Sometimes you have to be up against the wall before you can see that somebody already knocked a hole in it, and it is easy for you to walk right through it.

When you are faced with something that could turn out good but could also turn out bad, and there is no way to find out until you move forward, that is when you make the best educated guess you can (without being totally reckless) and then summon your courage and take the plunge. You must be willing to deal with things if they go bad. This requires courage, but when you are the one who goes for it, and it turns out well, then the goodness is yours.

Move forward and maintain momentum. The details of how your plan will work will be revealed with every step you take.

SECRET 44 - OPPORTUNITIES

P ractice and prepare in hopeful anticipation of opportunities, so when they arise, you are ready to act. The secret is: that the opportunities go to the people that have prepared and are ready to strike when opportunity knocks.

There are opportunities all around; to start businesses, to find solutions, to build relationships, to open doorways, to adapt, to lead. To make money, to make meaningful contributions, to learn, grow, and develop, to help others and to do the right thing. Opportunities give you ways to succeed.

All kinds of opportunities will present themselves if you keep looking. Often, success will appear in a different form than you expected; so, learn to be nimble and quick and to recognize opportunity when it appears. Practice and prepare, and then practice and prepare some more. Keep looking with expectation so you don't miss it. When a window of opportunity opens, seize it with a sense of urgency before the window closes.

SECRET 45 - OPTIMISM

Optimism is a form of faith that tells you that things will work out and be okay.

When you expect something to work out and you are thinking it, saying it, and believe it, it will come to pass, more often than not.

With this optimistic expectancy, the forces of the world will see your belief and expectancy and will line up to make it so.

Think of a dog that wants you to feed him. He is already excited and happy and thanking you with his body language, showing his optimism and his expectation he will be fed. Even if you were not thinking about feeding him before, now you probably are and are much more likely to feed him. This is how life is for optimists. Their optimism makes the world much more inclined to fulfill their expectations.

If you need water in the desert and have faith that you will find it, you will look longer and more creatively, and your chances will be many times greater than if you give up. If you believe you will get a promotion at work, you will act in a way that makes people think about promoting you. If you need healing, believe you will be healed. This will activate healing forces inside you.

A negative outlook closes doors, but a positive outlook opens doors and possibilities. Optimists look for the good in every situation and try to find the valuable lessons. Optimists are more open minded, so they try more things and learn more things and continue trying longer, increasing their chances of success.

SECRET 46 - OVERCOMING CHALLENGES

Why is it that we try to do the right things in life and be good people but sometimes bad things still happen to us? Could it be that God himself puts challenges in our life to help us grow stronger? Think about what life would be without any challenges or drama? Imagine a sporting event with no challenges. Pretty boring! Now imagine that life is like a sporting event. If you were handed a win every time with no challenges, you would grow weak. Maybe this is why we like games and sporting events so much, because something deep within us loves to face challenges, train, and overcome obstacles, ultimately achieving the goal after a hard-won fight.

If it is part of how we are wired, to love the feeling of overcoming obstacles and winning after a tough challenge. Then when life gives you a challenge, you will realize it's not the end of the world. It is only one more opportunity to grow stronger in your personal game of life. Then you can focus on developing the skills and mindset required to overcome challenges.

When you train hard, work hard, overcome challenges, and achieve your goal, you change into a stronger person. You become more confident, more capable, more fearless, more productive, and more able to succeed now and in the future.

Without the drama and challenge, your accomplishments would not be all that great, would they? So, hang in there, and be great.

SECRET 47 - PATHS TO SUCCESS

In high school, you are lucky if you have a general idea of what you want to do after you graduate. We are all different, and we all have different strengths. Many of us don't know what we want to do and must try several things before we find something that feels right. If you don't enjoy what you're doing, then try something else that feels more in line with your strengths. We often take whatever job we can get to make money just because we have to pay the bills. But don't settle there if that is not your true calling. If you know you were meant to do something else, something that gives you energy, something that motivates you, something that enthuses you, then pursue that. See if you can find a way to get paid for it. Even if it takes a long time to achieve it, pursue it. If you can find your sweet spot, where you love doing what you do, then success will come easier, and work will be a joy.

The paths you can take are endless, and success is not all about money, but here are a few common path ideas.

Trade school: A year or two of your time and money invested in a trade school will significantly increase your chances of getting a job in that trade.

College: If you invest money and years into college, it will probably help you get a job.

Self-education: Reading, researching, and studying any area of interest can make you an expert in that area. Experts tend to get paid more and create opportunities for themselves.

Create something: Invent, write, build, design, discover.

Use your talent: Whatever your talent is, if you develop it well, you may be able to use it to make money.

Get a part-time job: It will bring in money but also allow you time to develop other paths on the side.

Get a full-time job: This is the most common way to make money.

Start a part-time or full-time business: Owning a successful business is one of the most effective ways to create wealth.

Invest in rental property: Have you ever heard the old saying, "I live off the rents"?

Invest in the stock market: Have you ever heard the old saying, "I live off the dividends"?

These are just a few common path ideas to make money that you can use individually or in combination. Remember, if you can find your sweet spot where you love doing what you do, then success will come easier, and work will be a joy.

Even if you don't find your sweet spot, all paths can be honorable and lead to success, depending on the person you become and the performance you give. You are the path-picker and traveler. Don't be impatient. Travel steadily along the path, and become the best you can be on whatever path you pick, and you will succeed.

SECRET 48 - PERSEVERANCE

Life is full of ups, downs, obstacles, and setbacks. When pursuing your goals, decide in advance that you will never stop, and you will always bounce back. When you get knocked down by the waves of life, you won't get upset; you will get back up, learn from it, find solutions, and keep going. This is where people get stuck, when adversity shows up they stop, one day too soon or one obstacle too soon or just a few meters from the finish line. The secret is; you will succeed if you just don't stop.

Keep the big picture in mind. Are you moving in the right direction? Focus on taking as many steps forward as you can and protecting yourself from sliding back. Two steps forward and one back is okay if you are moving in the right general direction.

Perseverance is when you have the self-discipline to keep moving forward, until you finish. When you persevere, it boosts your self-esteem, and every step you take makes you stronger until you become unstoppable.

Keep going; you're closer than you think.

SECRET 49 - PERSONAL DEVELOPMENT

As we travel through life, we are constantly working on the ultimate "Do it yourself" project. That project is our lives.

If you don't grow, learn, and improve, then you will remain where you are with about the same as you have right now. If you want to move up and get more, you must continually improve your thinking, actions, knowledge, skills, and talents. The more you develop, improve, and grow, the more you will attract the good life to you.

For example, if you become more skillful and valuable at your job, you will probably get paid more. Careers, relationships, health —you can improve most areas of life if you work at it diligently.

Personal development is an investment in yourself. It is taking classes, going to seminars, reading books, and listening to motivational or instructional CDs in your car. It is about developing the mindset and habits that attract abundance. It is about developing the ability to do ordinary things better than you can do now.

The level of the good life you obtain is not dependent on others; it is dependent on your continual improvement. We attract what we want by making our knowledge, skills, and talents more attractive through personal development.

SECRET 50 - PLANS

W hen you have a goal or opportunity, you must take action if you want to achieve it. Wishing it to be so will not make it so; you must act.

Making a plan is a proven way to make your efforts to obtain or achieve something more successful. A good plan will map out the steps needed to do what you want to do.

The secret is; the person with the best plan is normally the most successful. It is a good idea to collaborate with others to make a good plan, because two or more people working together in harmony as a mastermind group will usually come up with the best plan.

Of course, things don't always go as planned, and if your plan is not working, then it is time to figure out why and adjust accordingly.

The plan doesn't have to be complete to the last detail, but it should be practical and workable. Any plan is better than no plan. Sometimes the only plan is to achieve the first step. When you do achieve the first step, you can change your focus to the next step, make another plan, and keep doing it for as long as it takes. You need to get moving and keep moving on the plan, even when it's not perfect. The details of your plan will be revealed with every step you take. Make your plan, act on it, and then follow through with persistence.

A plan is a tool to make your actions more intelligent. Taking intelligent action is a secret to success.

SECRET 51 - RELATIONSHIPS

Nobody succeeds to their full potential in isolation; there are always others that are contributing one way or another.

Good relationships will help bring you up and bad relationships will help bring you down.

Treat people the way you would want to be treated.

Pay attention.

Let people know you are there. Show up. Stand up.

Let people know you see them. Acknowledge them.

Let people know you hear them. Listen to them.

Act with honesty, kindness, and love.

Do the right thing, do it all the time.

Good relationships with people will move you forward, open doors, enhance your life, and bring you happiness. Good relationships are a secret to success.

SECRET 52 - RENTAL PROPERTIES

Owning rental properties is one of the most effective ways to create money that flows to you forever. If you buy a house and rent it to someone, then the house is creating income for you.

If you can rent it for more than the mortgage is costing you, then the house pays for itself and gives you a little extra money every month. However, if the mortgage is going to cost way more than you can rent the house for, it is probably wise not to buy it. Look at different properties. If you still can't find one that can pay for itself, forget the idea. The timing or the area might not be right.

If you find a property that pays for itself and makes a little extra every month, you can take that little extra every month and use it to pay off the mortgage early. When the mortgage goes away, the rents will provide a source of income that will put money in your pocket every month for the rest of your life.

Get one, two, or more properties, and suddenly your retirement income will be looking up.

It is easier than you think to get started. Just save a little money for a down payment, keep your day job, and maintain your credit rating. Then talk to a realtor or lender, and he or she will make it easy and help you get the property. You can manage the property yourself or hire a property manager.

Creating money that flows to you forever may be easier than you think.

SECRET 53 - REPETITION

You can obtain mental and physical power through repetition. Your muscles, mind, skills, talents, and abilities are all strengthened through repetitive use.

The more you do something, the better you get at it. If you want to be good at anything, do it repeatedly until you master it.

The secret is; the people you see that appear strong, skilled and talented did not start out with any more ability than you have. They have just developed those abilities, little by little, by doing the activity over and over again. It is a simple strategy, but it is also powerful.

SECRET 54 - RESPONSIBILITY

Do what you're supposed to do, even when nobody knows you're doing it. This is responsibility.

You will not be trusted with more until you show you are responsible with what you have.

It takes a long time to build trust—and a short time to lose it.

Opportunities and blessings seem to come automatically to responsible people.

Don't be lazy or careless, because the little things, if neglected, can be your downfall.

It is your responsibility to do your best with what you have wherever you are.

It is your responsibility to be who you are, to find and develop your gifts, and to discover your sweet spot, and try to be your best.

No excuses; take responsibility.

SECRET 55 - REST

Use rest as part of your success strategy.

Do not confuse rest with sleep. Sleep is a basic requirement, like eating right and exercising. Sleep recharges your system; it cleans toxins out of your brain and keeps you healthy and functioning properly. Getting enough sleep is a basic requirement; you need to get about seven or eight hours a night at regular times to stay at your best. You can't change your routine too much without your performance suffering.

Rest, on the other hand, can be inserted strategically to build strength and endurance and achieve more.

If you do all you can at a given time, does that mean you are done? No, if you rest a little, you can do more. After that you can rest again and do more. You can pretty much keep doing this strategy for as long as it takes to do whatever you are trying to achieve.

If you rest but then get back at it as soon as possible, this strategy will build your endurance and make you stronger each time and enable to do more and more at a given time while requiring less and less rest in between.

Slowing down is also a form of rest. Sometimes just slowing down for a little bit is enough to enable you to go hard again soon. When others burn out and stop, you will know that, with a little rest, you can do more. You are not done; you can go far beyond.

SECRET 56 - RUN YOUR OWN RACE

You are not someone else; you are you.

You can follow the paths of others and learn from people who have been there and done what you want to do, but when you travel the path, it is your race. You make it yours by giving meaning to the race that is your own. Your ability and your pace are yours. You don't need to beat everybody in the race; you only need to perform well compared to your personal best and try to improve on it.

The secret is; you are you. Own it.

SECRET 57 - SELF-DISCIPLINE

It is one thing to know what you should do, but it is another thing to actually do what you should do.

We are often lazy, unmotivated, distracted, and looking for any reason to do what is easy and put off the harder things. We like to do easy things that have immediate rewards.

The mark of a person who has matured mentally to the point of truly being in charge of his or her life is the ability to discipline his or her actions and to do what should be done, not just what is easy. Discipline doesn't normally produce immediate payback, but it is an investment that pays bigger rewards over time. Doing what you should do will make you feel good about yourself, and one good discipline leads to another. An investment in any good discipline tends to pay back in multiple ways.

Having the discipline to do what you should do when others are doing what is easy can be lonely, because if you tell others what you are doing, they might say "yeah good for you" but secretly be thinking, *Oh, you think you're better than the rest of us, don't you?*

Self-discipline is when you quietly do what you should do even when you don't feel like it and when no one is watching. People may not know the time and effort you put into doing what you should do, but your life will begin to shine as an example of success. People will wonder things like, *How are you doing better on the job? How did you get so good at things? How did you and your life get in such good shape?* Self-discipline is the quiet sport of champions.

SECRET 58 - SELF-MASTERY

You cannot always control the outer game. The outer game is what happens all around you, things like the cost of living, the political environment, the amount of taxes taken off your paycheck, the way a person offends you, the inevitable junk in life that you don't deserve but with which you still have to deal. You can do all the right things and act like a saint and still something or someone will give you a hard time and make your life difficult. We cannot always control the outer game.

However, you can try to control the inner game. The inner game is how you think and react to day-to-day conditions and the inevitable junk with which you are faced. When confronted with junk, you can do one of two things. The first option is to become a hothead and fight against the disruptions in your life, continually blaming or running away to try and find greener pastures with easier conditions. The problem with this approach is that so-called greener pastures come with a whole new set of problems and a new list of things on which to blame your hardships.

The other option is to work on your inner game. Learn to think and react better and function well in the wave of junk when it hits. The inner game is a mindset, a way of thinking that allows you to accept things that don't make sense and maintain your inner peace, thinking clearly and calmly and functioning with the best course of action in any given situation. Self-mastery may never be fully mastered, but you can learn to handle conditions better if you focus on the inner game.

Things like, forgive and forget. Look for the good in the situation and move on. Do what you should do, not just what is easy. Say or think affirmative thoughts like, "I am strong" and "I am able," .

Another part of self-mastery is to become the best you can be. One way to do this is to focus on what is truly good for you. For example, you don't forgive people to help them; you forgive, because it is good for you. You keep a good attitude, because it is good for you. You get eight hours of sleep, because it's good for you. You study, because it's good for you. You maintain peace of mind, because it is good for you. You treat others right, because it's good for you. You start good habits and stop bad habits, because good habits are good for you and bad habits are bad for you.

We may never totally master ourselves but if we pay attention we can improve some of the control over our thoughts, feelings, emotions, habits, and actions. it may be the ultimate challenge, but even a little self-mastery rewards you with more happiness, peace of mind, and success. The inner game is yours.

SECRET 59 - SELF-TALK

We all go around thinking private thoughts all day long. This is self-talk. If you control the inner dialogue by thinking about the direction you want the inner conversation to go and the topics on which you want to focus, then self-talk becomes a tool to control your life.

Self-talk is one of the most powerful determinants of success, because it will program your mind one way or another, whether or not you are paying attention. Your programmed mind is what you think and believe. If you're not paying attention to what you're saying to yourself, you might be programming thoughts and beliefs that are hurting you.

You program your mind with what you think and say to yourself most often, because what you experience most is what you end up believing most.

If you are constantly thinking and saying good and positive things to yourself and about yourself, then you will tend to have a good and positive life. But beware, the opposite is also true.

Say and think things to yourself like, "I am strong. I am smart. I can and will get a promotion. I will succeed at this. This is a good thing." Say these or any other statement you want to be true.

Thinking and saying things like this over and over in your mind is the secret. The power to program your brain comes from repeating the statement about your life that you want to be true until your brain builds a new connection that allows you to believe it. The new connection is the new program. This process will improve your self-image and build your confidence, and it will mysteriously draw in the things you need in life to make it true. You become what you think and say you are.

Self-talk is the tool to program your brain into believing who you are, what you do, and where you are going. Belief becomes reality, and you actually become what you say, think, and believe.

This is the power of self-talk

SECRET 60 - SOWING AND REAPING

S owing is planting seeds, and reaping is harvesting what you plant.

A law of nature says the amount you sow determines how much you will reap. If you plant a lot of corn, you will harvest a lot of corn. This law applies not only to planting food but also to everything you do in life. Everything you do produces something in direct proportion to how much you do. If you do a lot, you get a lot. Do a little, get a little. There is no free ride. You determine how much success you receive.

If you want more, do more. Work more, build more, construct more, achieve more, help more, organize more, and learn more. Have more enthusiasm, more imagination, more faith, and more persistence.

If your service is more valuable, your product is more useful, or you help more people, you will have more profits, more success, and more riches in direct proportion to how much more you give and do.

SECRET 61 - SIMPLICITY

Keeping things simple is a key to success.
Don't be overwhelmed by how much of anything is going on. Keep things simple, and focus on what works.

If you have an idea you want to work, make the idea as simple as possible. Make it simple to explain, easy to understand, simple to do, and easy to implement. We tend to overcomplicate things. If something is too complicated, you won't embrace it, and neither will others.

We learn a lot of things over time, but that doesn't mean we should do all those things or think about all those things at the same time. If you try to think about or do too many things at once, it will drive you crazy. For happiness, peace of mind, and success, focus on one thing at a time, and keep everything simple. Do one simple thing, and when that is done, do another simple thing, and so on.

SECRET 62 - SKILLS

Nobody is born with skills; people must learn them one at a time.

The secret is; that very often it only takes one new skill to thrust you to a whole new level of income and success.

Can you identify any skills that if mastered, would thrust you to a new level of success?

If others can learn new skills, so can you.

Sure you will have to pay the price, with time and effort but you can learn it. You can do it.

One skill at a time, you can rise to the top.

SECRET 63 - SPECIALTY

I f you become a master at something, you can have great success in that field.

If you want to improve your lot in life, try to get better at whatever you do. We all find ourselves in one place or another, doing one thing or another. When you look around, you will see some people who are doing very well, and some who are struggling under the same conditions. Does the person who is thriving, function better as the result of some miracle? No, he or she has just learned and trained more in the specialty that is required for that particular environment.

Take a person who has not learned to swim and drop him or her in the water, and that person will struggle. However, a trained swimmer can have fun and make things look easy under the same conditions.

Is thriving in your environment a miracle? No, it is a result of education and training and working day in and day out at perfecting your craft. Improve yourself regarding what you do, and the specialty that is required to rise to the top in your environment, and you will succeed.

To be one of the best, strive continuously to get better. If you barely learn to function and never try to improve after that, then you will remain at that level. The best work at mastering their craft day in and day out, and they are rewarded accordingly.

SECRET 64 - THE STOCK MARKET

The most common way for people in America to gain wealth is to start a retirement/investment account, like an IRA (Individual Retirement Account) or 401k. If you set up an account that automatically invests part of your income in the account each month, then you will learn to live on the rest of your income and not miss the money that goes into your investments.

Most of us don't have the discipline to save and invest money every month, so the secret is to make the investment automatic. You can set up the account to invest in stocks, bonds, mutual funds, or whatever you choose. If you invest money automatically every month, the amount will grow, compound, and, given enough time, you will become wealthy. How wealthy you become will be determined by how much you put in the account every month, what kind of return or appreciation the investment produces, and how much time it has to grow. For most of us, picking stocks is a 50/50 chance and very difficult, so it is easier to go with established mutual funds that follow the overall market and stick with it for the long run. Of course, sometimes the funds go down in value, and there is risk involved with any investment, but if you are in it for the long run, it will work most of the time. If your employer offers a retirement account, that is a good place to start. If your employer offers to match the amount you put in the account, take advantage of it, because it is like free money. If you don't have that option from an employer, set up your own IRA.

Invest as much as you can, let it grow over time, and you will become wealthy automatically.

SECRET 65 - STRESS

E veryone gets stressed, but managing stress is vital to performing at your best.

A lot of stress is self-induced; we put too much pressure on ourselves. Keep things in perspective. Few situations are a truly life-or-death crisis. Do your best, but remember things always work out one way or another, and in most cases, nobody is going to die.

You can strengthen your ability to deal with stress by doing stress-relieving activities and hobbies, such as exercising, playing sports, or doing relaxing hobbies, like gardening, playing guitar, or watching funny shows on television. Getting enough sleep and eating healthy food also strengthens your resistance to stress. Fresh air and sunshine help, too. If you do some of these things regularly, you will be stronger and avoid getting stressed too easily.

When you do get stressed, slow down, take some deep breaths, and step back. Remind yourself it is not a life-or-death crisis, and you will get through it. Remember it could be worse. Choose to be an optimist. Trust that even though things may not work out the way you want, some good will come of it. If nothing else, it will make you grow stronger for next time.

If you take some of these mental and physical steps, you will not eliminate stress but you will manage stress better than others, and this can give you the edge in becoming a top performer.

SECRET 66 - SUCCESS

S uccess is defined by your values and what you say success is to you, but it is also something that you achieve.

The answer to how to achieve your goals has already been found. Find an example of what others have used to get what you want, and then do what they did. Pay the price they have paid, follow the recipe they followed, and you will get the same or similar results.

Any success you have or don't have is largely a matter of sowing and reaping. You will harvest what you plant. No apologies, no complaints. Your success is a direct result of what you do.

SECRET 67 - THE LAW OF RECIPROCITY

The law of reciprocity is an invisible force that makes people want to pay other people back for the good or bad they do.

If you do something good for someone, they will want to do something good for you. It is not required that they do something good for you, and you should not expect it, but an invisible force in the back of their mind will subtly suggest it is okay and that maybe they should. The same is true if you do something bad. Others will be inclined to treat you the same way.

The law of reciprocity seems to work best when you do good with no expectation of reward. If you do good and expect something in return, then it becomes a form of manipulation, and people will sense that you are not genuinely good and will be inclined to treat you that way.

So, the secret is to do good. If you do good everywhere you go, then good will follow you everywhere you go.

SECRET 68 - THE MIND

We have a conscious mind, the mind that is aware of thoughts that get our attention, but we also have a subconscious mind that is continually generating thoughts that don't get our attention but have a huge impact on us one way or another.

Deep within our subconscious are the accumulated memories of every experience, conversation, TV show, and person we have ever met, everything we have heard, seen, felt, said, or done.

This accumulated input is one secret source from which thoughts come. Every bit of input your mind has experienced is in there, generating thought vibrations that attract other, similar thought vibrations, whether good or bad.

Some of these hidden thoughts vibrate stronger than others, because we have experienced them more often or in a stronger way. The more we experience something, and the deeper we experience it, the more dominant the thought-generating force will be. The stronger the experience, the stronger the subconscious is affected. This is why experiences involving strong emotions or strong beliefs tend to dominate our hidden thoughts.

So, here is the secret: Control the input. Negative attracts negative, so limit negative input. Positive attracts positive, so input more positive thoughts. You can decide from this day forward what your new, dominating thoughts will be by continually inputting the thoughts you want to grow and multiply. If you want prosperity, think prosperous thoughts. If you want good health, think healthy thoughts. If you want happiness, think happy thoughts. The way to make these or any other thoughts more dominant in your life is to make the input stronger and more frequent. Think about it continually, and mix it with emotions and beliefs.

Your subconscious will attract ideas, insights, plans, opportunities, and other thoughts that are similar to whatever you have been inputting.

Load in the thoughts in which you want your subconscious to work, and powerful things will start to happen for you.

SECRET 69 - THOUGHTS

This will probably sound far out to most people, but let's say it is possible just for a minute, that thoughts are some kind of living things. They have a life of their own. They have lived before us and they will still be here when we are gone. They are an invisible force that creates the visible. Thoughts come to your mind and, in effect, say, "Do you want to be my friend, hang out, experience life and do something together?" Now, you have a choice, to hang out with the thought and experience what it has to offer; or not. If you like the thought you can spend some time with it and if you start to believe in it then you can become a co-creator with it. The thought is the leader that says it wants to create something or do something, and you are the worker who helps bring the creation or action to life.

When you truly believe in a thought, the thought works to bring itself to life. It will bring to you advanced wisdom and insights and show you the way, empowering and emboldening you, and somehow providing all you need to bring it to life and make it real. The thought requires you and your belief, and you require the thought.

If life comes from life and the thought just physically manifested itself through you, is the thought alive? Is it experiencing life through us? Who knows? OK, maybe a little far out. But the point is; that thoughts should be given respect and taken seriously because they contain immense power.

Here is the secret: Your life follows your thoughts. But you control what thoughts you believe and hang out with.

You tend to become what you believe you will become.

You tend to get what you believe you will get.

You tend to do what you believe you will do.

You tend to create what you believe you will create.

If you choose which thoughts to believe and hang out with, your life will follow, you will be forcing life in the direction you choose. If you keep forcing life in the direction you choose long enough, you will tend to get what you want and get where you want to be.

SECRET 70 - TIME MANAGEMENT

"Early to bed early to rise makes you healthy, wealthy, and wise." When you get up early, full of energy, and get started while the average person is still sleeping, you automatically have an edge.

Don't waste time. Everything you do matters, and everything adds up one way or another. If you spend time on high-value activities that move you closer to your goals, and make your life better, you will be ahead of the time wasters.

Plan your day in advance. If you already know where you are going, you will get there faster.

Do the hardest thing first. Do whatever is most valuable and important. Focus until it's done. When you're done, use that feeling of accomplishment as momentum to finish other tasks.

Develop a sense of urgency. Do not delay or procrastinate. Do it while the sense of "you should be doing it now" is upon you. If you delay, your mind will talk you out of it. The faster you move, the more you will accomplish. The more you get done, the more success you will have.

Time is like money, it can be invested. If you invest your money you are looking to get the best return (rewards) on investment that you can. If you are managing time effectively you are also looking to get the best return (rewards) on time invested that you can. Time has value. The secret is to recognize the value and not waste it.

SECRET 71 - VALUE

How much are you worth? To you and your family, you are priceless. You are worth more than any amount of money.

How much somebody is willing to pay you is another matter. Your employer will not pay you whatever you think you deserve just because you think you are worth it. Your employer will pay you according to the value you bring to the company or organization. The world will not pay you just because you think it should. The world will pay you only for what you bring that is of value to others.

If you see somebody getting paid more than you, it's usually because that person is bringing more value to others than you are. Maybe the person is bringing more skills, knowledge, leadership ability, organizational ability, faith, vision, enthusiasm, persistence, hard work, or perhaps just a better attitude.

It is a mistake to think that life is unfair and others just got lucky. When you improve your skills, service, knowledge, abilities, offerings, attitudes, and all the things that bring value to others, that's when you outgrow the old perception others have of you, and people naturally see you have more value to offer and are willing to pay you more.

SECRET 72 - VISUALIZATION

The starting point of achieving your dream is to see your dream happening in your mind. This is visualization. Visualize in detail the dream happening perfectly in every way. Go through the steps, see it going well, and see it happening.

Visualizing something happening is like practicing before the event. The secret is; that it is a form of rehearsal that will sharpen your skills and build your confidence.

Confidence will enable you to act, and your actions will be better because they have been rehearsing in your mind. If you can see it, you can do it.

Visualization is one of the secret tools of success.

SECRET 73 - WEAKNESS

We all have areas of weakness. There are some things we are not good at, have no discipline with, or struggle with physically. If you just say to yourself, "Oh well, that's just the way it is," then you will be destined to live with your weakness and suffer accordingly the rest of your life. The other option is to make at least some improvement in your area of weakness. If your back is weak, do back exercises. If you have trouble cooking, read some recipe books or watch cooking shows. If you need to improve at anything, start working on it, little by little. By spending some time now, fixing what needs fixing and improving what needs improving, you can diminish or eliminate your weaknesses one by one. You will never be strong in everything, but you can be better at some things. Some things are worth the time and effort to improve. When you suffer because of a weakness, that is a sign you need to put in some time and effort to improve that area of your life. Don't ignore the sign and the opportunity to do something about it. A little time and effort now can yield a lifetime of benefits.

SECRET 74 - WORK

The secret is; it takes hard work to succeed. Being lazy is for losers.

The more work you do, the more success you will have. It is that simple.

If you start a little earlier, work a little harder, work a little better, work a little smarter, and stay a little later, your success is all but guaranteed.

When you work, don't fool around, and don't waste time. Do the big, important tasks first.

Think of yourself as self-employed even if you are not. Take responsibility for doing the work like you own the company.

Commit to being the best you can be. Strive to be in the top 10 percent of achievers in your field. Do the extra work to become excellent at what you do. Pay the price, make the sacrifices, and put in the time to achieve mastery.

Time is going by one way or another. If you use your time to work hard and strive for excellence, over time, you will rise to the top.

Success hides behind work. When you work hard, you attract success, and it will show itself. You must pay the price in advance before success comes to you. People think they can just go through the buffet line of life and point to an item they want, and someone will hand it to them, but that is not how life works. If you want something, you must plant the crop, water it, and tend to it; then the harvest will show itself to you. After you do the work.

SECRET 75 - YOU

Y ou are special.

Can you imagine what a miracle it is that, in the entire universe, you were even born at all, that you are living, thinking, and capable of making decisions? Add to that the fact that your fingerprints and DNA are unique. No other human who has ever lived—or who will ever live—is exactly like you. You are special.

You might not always be proud of what you do, but you can always be proud of who you are. You are a miracle. You are special. You are unique. You have gifts that no others possess. You are special in the city, and you are special in the country. You are special on the mountain, and you are special in the valley. You are special if you have a lot, and you are special if you have a little. You are special if you know where you're going or if you are lost. No matter where you are in life, you are special.

AFTERWORD

One last secret is; that life generally will not get any easier. But it will appear to get easier as we get better and stronger and more able to provide for ourselves. When you are a baby, waking is hard, but as you get better, it seems easy. When you get a little older reading may seem hard, but as you learn it seems easy. Getting around town on foot is hard but when you are able to provide yourself with a car it gets easier. The challenges we encounter, like making money, dealing with people, understanding things that make very little sense and every other challenge, have always been hard; at first. But we do get better, stronger and more able as we go. My hope is that this little book has given you some insights that you have found to be true or helpful. Giving you that little extra empowerment to guide yourself, and speed up the process of getting stronger and more able. The power has always been in you. You have the power to make life appear at least a little easier. If you forget everything else just try to do the right thing and do it all the time.

May you all live long, healthy, happy, prosperous lives.

ACKNOWLEDGMENTS

I thank my parents for setting a good example, I thank my children for being a source of inspiration, I thank my wife for her love and support, I thank all those people in history that have helped bring this secret wisdom to light, I thank Kevin Miller for his editorial contributions and I thank God.

Thanks to Rick Lakin at iCrew Digital Publishing for his publishing, marketing, and website services. The cover was designed by DJ Rogers at justwritedesign.com.

ABOUT THE AUTHOR

Frank Leigh made his journey from lack to abundance only after he discovered that the secrets to success were not what he thought they were. Those findings are revealed in this book. He is a successful investor and business owner. He is a part time inventor, writer, musician and runner. He is 56 years old, with grown children and young grandchildren and lives with his loving wife and 2 dogs in Hemet, California

Read more about Frank and his books at CanandWill.com.

Made in the USA
San Bernardino, CA
14 March 2018